ISBN 978-0-260-83281-8
PIBN 10974521

PRESENT STATE

OF

MARYLAND.

BY THE

DELEGATES OF THE PEOPLE.

Maryland, General assembly. 1787. House of de

BALTIMORE PRINTED:

LONDON REPRINTED;

FOR JOHN STOCKDALE, OPPOSITE BURLINGTON HOUSE,
PICCADILLY,

M DCC LXXXVII.

[Price One Shilling.]

Copy 2

TO THE

P E O P L E

O F

M A R Y L A N D.

WE, your immediate reprefentatives in the general affembly, think ourfelves refponfible to you for our conduct, and that on all fubjects that materially concern your welfare or happinefs, you are to be confulted; and your opinions, freely and fairly delivered, ought to govern our deliberations.

We alfo hold both branches of your legiflature bound by your inftructions, whenever you pleafe to give them; on a diverfity in fentiment between us and the fenate, you alone are to decide, and to you only can there be any appeal.

We wifh you to be truly informed of the fituation of your affairs, and however critical or dangerous, we have a confidence in your virtue, fortitude and perfeverance, and that you will never defpair of the

A 2 public

public fafety. Duty and inclination, and a defire to receive your approbation of our conduct, induce us to communicate to you the real ftate of your government at this time, and the meafures propofed by us to afford the beft relief, we conceive, in your power to give.

We fhall not enter into the detail, but briefly exhibit, in one view, the proportion of this ftate of the federal expences, *in time of peace,* which ftands thus :

                                           Dollars.

    1. The expences of Congrefs *civil* eftablifhment for 1786   -   -   446,876

    2. Intereft of Congrefs *foreign* debt for 1786   -   -   -   -   1,723,626

                                    2,170,502

Suppofe, the proportion of this ftate one tenth, (though in our opinion above it) is 217,050 dollars, equal to £81,267 : 12 : 6 current money. This fum can only be paid in *fpecie.*

    3. Intereft of Congrefs *domeftic* debt for 1786, 1,606,566 dollars.

Suppofe the proportion of this ftate one tenth, is 160,656 dollars, equal to £60,621 current money. Congrefs *domeftic* debt confifted of continental loan-office certificates, of which this ftate has liquidated (and funded by the confolidating act) to the amount of £80,517 : 4 : 9, the annual intereft of which being £4,831 : 0 : 4, deducted from £60,621, leaves a

                                        balance

balance of £55,789 : 19 : 8, which muſt alſo be paid
in ſpecie, unleſs this ſtate can pay the balance of
former requiſitions, which Congreſs ſtate (on 30th
June 1786) at 965,851 dollars; in which caſe it
may be diſcharged in certificates (called *indents*)
granted for intereſt due on continental govern-
mental ſecurities. The *condition* of paying this balance of former requiſitions, is abſolutely out of
the power of the ſtate, and if it was in its power,
we have no means to procure the continental ſecurities.

4. The proportion of this ſtate of the intereſt of
Congreſs foreign and domeſtic debt, is really, and
muſt *for ever* remain, until we obtain continental
ſecurities, at £137,057 : 12 : 2 ſpecie.

5. To the civil eſtabliſhment of 1786, Congreſs,
by their requiſition of 20th October laſt, have called
on this ſtate to pay, before the 20th June next,
49,979 dollars, equal to £ 18741 : 2 : 6.

6. If this ſtate can make no proviſion for the
intereſt of Congreſs *domeſtic* debt, its proportion of
Congreſs *foreign* debt, and civil eſtabliſhment for
1786, will amount to £ 100,008 : 15 : 0 ſpecie.

From this ſtate it evidently appears, that this
government ought, if poſſible, to raiſe above
£ 100,000 for Congreſs for the year 1786, and that
too without the leaſt proviſion for our proportion of
the intereſt of Congreſs *domeſtic* debt.

The annual expences of our own government
may be eſtimated at £ 16,000 ſpecie. It is ſup-

posed that the whole, or the far greater part of our state debt, is funded by bonds for confiscated British property, except a debt we owe Messieurs Vanstaphorst of £ 45,700 : 4 : 7 current money, with interest to 1st September, 1786.

The property in this state *assessed* may be estimated at £ 10,000,000 currency. If the whole demands were to be raised on the assessed property, it would require on every hundred pounds thereof about   -   -   1 : 3 : 4

To this must be added the county
tax, supposed   -   -   5 : 0
_____
£ 1 : 8 : 4

We deliberated whether the sum of £ 116,000 specie could be collected from you in the space of one year, and whether you could constantly and perpetually pay at least that sum annually.

In the course of our inquiry, as to your ability to pay such an annual perpetual tax, we took a general view of the present situation of your trade, and we also reflected on your private circumstances.

The imports since the peace are great, and a very considerable part of them consists of luxuries, and, from the best information we could procure, may be estimated at £ 600,000 current money.

The exports consist wholly of your produce, and we state them thus:

25,000

25,000 hogsheads of tobacco, at
£ 15 current money per hogshead, £375,000 : 0 : 0
700,000 bushels of wheat, or
140,000 barrels of flour, above con-
sumption, at 6s. 8d. per bushel,   133,333 : 6 : 8
Indian corn and lumber   -   30,000 : 0 : 0

£538,333 : 6 : 8

These exports would require 31 vessels of the
burthen of 400 hogsheads of tobacco each, and 35
vessels of 2000 barrels of flour each, navigated by
792 seamen and mariners, every vessel making two
voyages to Europe within the year; and we have
not above one-third of that quantity of shipping or
mariners belonging to this state.

The debts due by you to Great-Britain before
the war, we believe may amount to about £ 600,000
sterling.

The debts due to Great-Britain since the peace,
is supposed to be about £ 400,000 sterling.

The debts due from you, *on interest*, to individuals within the state, may be estimated at about
£ 350,000 current money.

The debt due from you to the state, on bonds
for confiscated British property, and pledged to
state creditors, is £ 275,600 : 3 : 1.

The great number of suits in the general courts,
and in the several county courts, by British and
domestic creditors, for the recovery of very large
sums

fums of money, convinced us of the inability of many of you to fatisfy thefe creditors ; and we know that above 800 executions were iffued againft the *ftate* debtors to the laft general court, to compel the payment of the intereft then due to the ftate.

It appeared to this Houfe, that the arrearages of taxes, on the weftern fhore, for 1784, amounted to £ 22,495 : 7 : 6, and on the eaftern fhore, for 1784, to £6,122 : 16 : 8½; and that the arrearages of taxes on the weftern fhore, for 1785, amounted to £ 52,398 : 0 : 3, and on the eaftern fhore, for 1785, to £16,304 : 10 : 1½. Total of arrearages, for 1784 and 1785, £97,320 : 14 : 7. No return has been made by the commiffioners of the tax for 1786, but the amount may be eftimated at £ 100,000.—The whole of the arrearages of taxes, therefore, now due, are £ 197,320 : 14 : 7.

It is reprefented to this ftate by the board of treafury, in their letter of the 30th November, 1786, that the *furplus* of the receipt by Congrefs, from all the ftates, beyond what was neceffary to defray the charges of the government, in the courfe of two and an half years, that is, from the 31ft December, 1783, to the 30th June, 1786, was only 39,032 dollars, to be applied towards the dif-charge of the fpecie engagements unfatisfied in 1782 and 1783; and the board obferved, that unlefs the feveral ftates adopted, without delay, a more effici-ent mode of fupplying the general treafury than hitherto adopted, the confederacy of the ftates, on

which

4

which their exiſtence, as an independent people, too probably depended, *muſt inevitably be diſſolved*.

The reſult of our opinions on this inquiry was, that you could not diſcharge your *private* and your *public* engagements; and that you muſt neglect your *private* obligations, or your *public* duty. For if you paid your *debts*, you would thereby be unable to diſcharge your *taxes*; and if you paid your taxes, you muſt thereby be rendered unable to diſcharge your debts. Your honour, welfare and ſafety, required that every exertion ſhould be made to ſupport the union. We thought it imprudent and uſeleſs to lay on you *further* taxes, unleſs ſome *expedient* could be deviſed to aſſiſt you in the payment of them, and alſo in the diſcharge of your private debts.—In every ſtate there ought to be as much circulating money as will repreſent all the property and labour bought and ſold for caſh; and the current money of every country ought always to be in proportion to its trade, induſtry, conſumption, alienation *and taxes.*—If government wants to borrow from, or to increaſe the taxes on, its citizens, it is neceſſary to uſe all poſſible means to augment the quantity of money in circulation, in proportion to the ſum wanted on loan, or to be raiſed by taxes. We are convinced that there is not a ſufficient quantity of circulating ſpecie in this ſtate to anſwer the purpoſes of commerce alone, becauſe the chief produce of the country, tobacco and wheat, cannot command a reaſonable and proper price; becauſe

lands,

lands, houfes and negroes, will not fell for one half their actual value; and becaufe fpecie cannot be borrowed unlefs at an exorbitant premium (from 20 to 30 per cent.) to carry on trade or manu-factures, to build veffels, or to cultivate or improve our lands. It is difficult to afcertain the amount of fpecie in circulation in this ftate, and not lefs diffi-cult to determine what quantity is neceffary as a medium of commerce. We do not confider the trade of the ftate, at this time, in a more flourifh-ing condition than before the war; and we do not think at any time before that period, that the cir-culating fpecie exceeded £ 200,000; the objects of commerce far exceeded that fum, and the refidue was fupplied by paper money and credit. We know that in 1776, above £ 238,000 in bills of credit, emitted by the old government, and above £ 200,000 iffued by the conventions, were in cir-culation, and paffed until Auguft 1776, at par with fpecie. From this fact we draw thefe inferences, that the trade of this ftate, before the war, required a large fum of paper money to fupply the deficiency of fpecie; and if our commerce is nearly the fame at this time, as before the war, that even for that purpofe the fame quantity of paper may be emitted; and that if taxes increafe the demand, the fum may be augmented according to fuch additional demand. There are no mines of gold and filver in this ftate, and therefore we can only procure thofe metals by the export of the *produce* of our lands, as we have

no

no *manufactures*. The balance of trade being againſt us, for that cauſe we export, and do not import ſpecie. As there is certainly not a ſufficient quantity of gold and ſilver for a *medium* of *trade*, and for the *purpoſe* of *taxation*, we were of opinion, that a part of the *ſolid* or *real* property of our citizens, equal to the deficiency, might be *melted* down and made to circulate in paper money or bills of credit.

To explain and familiarize this idea of melting down and circulating *real* property in paper, we would ſuppoſe that the real property belonging to the citizens of this ſtate is actually worth 15,000,000*l.* ſpecie, that they owe for the public debt 1,000,000*l.* and the circulating gold and ſilver is only 200,000*l.* Gold and ſilver is the common ſtandard to meaſure the value of all commodities, and are called the *repreſentatives* or *ſigns* of wealth : It is evident that fifteen millions can diſcharge one, but if all the £ 200,000 could be collected by *taxes*, there would remain a balance of £ 800,000. How ſhall this balance be paid ? Your property is worth above fifteen times that ſum, and yet you muſt be *inſolvent as to taxes*, if no mode can be deviſed to procure ſome repreſentative of this property, *other* than gold and ſilver, which from its nature can circulate and anſwer *in taxes* the purpoſes of coin. The preſſure of taxes, is leſs intolerable from the amount, than the ſcarcity of a *medium* in which to pay them. Gold and ſilver is not only the *medium* of *trade*, but alſo of *taxes*. We think there is not near enough

of

tribute part of your property to fupport the federal union, and your own government, if you could be furnifhed with the means.

We have before ftated, that the proportion of the annual intereft of Congrefs *domeftic* debt, (after deducting the intereft of the fum liquidated by this ftate) amounts to £50,762 : 17 : 11¼. It is felf-evident, if this government can pay no part of this intereft, that it will be impoffible for us ever to difcharge the principal, with fuch an annual accumulating intereft. At this time the final fettlements, and other fecurities, iffued by Congrefs, bearing intereft, may be purchafed from fix to eight for one. It is apparent, that lefs than £200,000 fpecie, at this time, (and moft probable for a confiderable time hence) will purchafe above £1,000,000 of liquidated continental fecurities. It appears to us, therefore, prudent and wife to make great exertions to procure the *means* of purchafing thefe fecurities in their depreciated ftate. The governments having lands to fell, have procured with them great quantities of thefe fecurities; it was *one* of the great objects of our propofed emiffion, to apply part of the fum received in taxes, or part of the fum not circulated on loan, to this purpofe; if, as we expect, our paper fhould maintain its value at par with fpecie, or with a very little or trifling difference, it might either purchafe thefe fecurities, or tobacco or flour, which might be exchanged for them. We alfo expected, that part of the £100,000

not

of thefe metals for the *former*, and we are confident none of them for the *latter*. Our attention, therefore, has been given to devife fome *medium for taxes*; and none occurs to us fo proper and neceffary as a paper money, and we reafoned thus; if lands, the moft permanent and valuable of all property, can be mortgaged, and notes, or bills of credit, iffued on fuch fecurity, fuch notes, or bills of credit, would be the *fubftitute* or *reprefentative* of fuch land, in the fame manner as gold and filver is the reprefentative of land and all other property; and thefe notes would poffefs all the qualities of a circulating medium of trade, as well as coin, and muft have a real and intrinfic worth, as long as the lands, on which they iffue, retain their value. Gold and filver has been called the *high way*, which carries the produce of a country to market. We think, in like manner, paper money (if there is not fufficient of thofe metals) may be the vehicle to convey the property of the ftate, by *taxes*, into the public treafury; and, in our opinion, this paper money will anfwer *that purpofe* as well as gold and filver. Many of you who owe taxes have real property; but no fpecie; you have land, which is as much actual wealth as gold and filver; you cannot pay your land in taxes, or fell it for fpecie, but at a lofs of one-third or one half its real worth; if you could on a mortgage of part of your land obtain what would anfwer for taxes, you would readily borrow.—We doubt not your inclination to con-
tribute

tribute part of your property to fupport the federal union, and your own government, if you could be furnifhed with the means.

We have before ftated, that the proportion of the annual intereft of Congrefs *domeftic* debt, (after deducting the intereft of the fum liquidated by this ftate) amounts to £50,762 : 17 : 11¼. It is felf-evident, if this government can pay no part of this intereft, that it will be impoffible for us ever to difcharge the principal, with fuch an annual accumulating intereft. At this time the final fettlements, and other fecurities, iffued by Congrefs, bearing intereft, may be purchafed from fix to eight for one. It is apparent, that lefs than £200,000 fpecie, at this time, (and moft probable for a confiderable time hence) will purchafe above £1,600,000 of liquidated continental fecurities. It appears to us, therefore, prudent and wife to make great exertions to procure the *means* of purchafing thefe fecurities in their depreciated ftate. The governments having lands to fell, have procured with them great quantities of thefe fecurities; it was *one* of the great objects of our propofed emiffion, to apply part of the fum received in taxes, or part of the fum not circulated on loan, to this purpofe; if, as we expect, our paper fhould maintain its value at par with fpecie, or with a very little or trifling difference, it might either purchafe thefe fecurities, or tobacco or flour, which might be exchanged for them. We alfo expected, that part of the £100,000

I   not

not appropriated for loan to individuals, would be borrowed by several of our counties, for the purpose of laying out and making the capital roads, by which the produce of the back country is brought down, and exported from George-town and Baltimore town, a great and necessary business, and which calls loudly for legislative assistance.

On this review of your circumstances, public and private, to enable you to pay such taxes as the exigencies of the federal union and your own government required, and with a view of furnishing the means to secure a quantity of continental securities, we proposed to emit bills of credit to the amount of £350,000 current money, and to circulate £250,000, part thereof, on loan at six per cent. interest, on ample landed security of above double the value.—We appropriated £100,000 for loan to the inhabitants of the several counties, for 30 days after the money was ready for loan, (according to the property and taxes of each county): the sum to the largest county being £11,500, and to the smallest £1,700.—No loan to be less than £50, and not more than £500 to the same person. After the expiration of the 30 days, any money not lent out as appropriated, to be lent to any inhabitant of the state, in sums not less than £50, nor more than £1000; and not more than £1000 to the same person.—If this £100,000 was lent out, six months thereafter, the treasurer was authorized, with the approbation of the governor and council, to appropriate

priate and lend out the further fum of £50,000, in the fame manner. If this fum was alfo loaned, three months thereafter, a further fum of £50,000 might be appropriated, with the like approbation, and lent out in the fame manner; if this fum was alfo borrowed, three months thereafter, a further fum of £50,000 might be appropriated, with the like approbation, and loaned in the fame manner. The bill provided, that not more than £200,000 fhould be in circulation at the fame time, unlefs the governor and council fhould be fully fatisfied, that the loaning a further fum would not in any manner affect the value of the fum then in circulation. The bill directed, that the fix per cent. intereft, and one twentieth part of the debt, fhould be paid annually, and that one half of the intereft, and the one-twentieth part of the debt, fhould be annually funk, and the other half of the intereft fhould be lent. The bill declared, that the emiffion fhould *not* be a *tender* in law or equity, for any *paft* or *future* debt for money, unlefs fo agreed by the parties; and that the emiffion fhould not continue in circulation more than ten years; the bills of credit were to be received in payment of *all taxes and duties* due fince March 1784, or to be impofed during the time the faid bills fhall remain in circulation; and in payment of all county affeffments, falaries of officers of government, officers and attornies fees, &c. &c. but not in payment of five per cent. duties when impofed by Congrefs.—This

is

is the fubftance of the bill; further particulars are contained in the abftract we directed to be pub_lifhed for your information.

By this fcheme, not more than £250,000 could be put into circulation in the fpace of 12 months; and a debtor for £100, (if he paid his intereft and one-twentieth part of his debt annually) at the expiration of nine years, would pay £36 : 19 : 6, and he would owe the ftate £63 : 0 : 6. By this plan, if £100 is lent, and one-twentieth part thereof and fix per cent. is paid, annually, and the one-twentieth, and one-half the intereft, is funk annually, at the expiration of nine years, the one-twentieth will bring into the treafury £41 : 11 : 3; the fix per cent. will bring in £49 : 17 : 5; there will be funk £66 : 10 : 0¼ of the principal; there will remain in circulation only £33 : 9 : 11¾; there will be £91 : 8 : 8 principal and intereft paid in; there will be due to the ftate, with the accumulated intereft, £83 : 7 : 5¾; and the ftate will gain £49 : 17 : 6; and if the debtor and his fecurities fhould all prove to be worth nothing, the ftate could lofe only £8 : 11 : 4 of the original fum of £100. This will appear by the paper annexed, No. 1.—The paper annexed, No. 2, will alfo fhew a true ftate of the emiffion of £250,000, agreeably to the plan of our bill, the fum funk and in circulation, every year, and the profit to government.

This Houfe intended to fufpend the collection of the arrearages of taxes (before ftated to be
£197,320

£197,320.: 14 : 7) until £100,000 of the emiſſion
could be fully in circulation, on loan, in every part
of the ſtate; and at no time would the paper-money
in circulation be equal to the amount of the taxes.
We alſo intended to impoſe on you, for the ſup-
plies of 1787, a tax not exceeding 30/0 for every
hundred pounds worth of your property, and to
continue the ſame for ſeveral years; and to enable
you to pay this tax, we intended, by purchaſing
your produce, to circulate among you the amount,
or nearly the amount of the taxes, after paying the
expences of this government. We hoped and expected, that you would readily ſubmit to this taxation, and cheerfully exert yourſelves to pay it,
when furniſhed, in great meaſure, with the means,
and when you muſt clearly ſee, that by ſuch exertion
you would relieve yourſelves from a *perpetual* burthen, or a continental bankruptcy.

You will diſcover, from a deliberate attention to
your affairs, that you are in a moſt critical and
dangerous ſituation, and that ſome expedient ought
to be immediately adopted, that affords ſome proſ-
pect of relief. If we remain inactive, and neglect
to take deciſive meaſures, certain political ruin muſt
ſoon follow. No mode occurred to us ſo proper
as an emiſſion of paper money, and you will ſee,
that the ſcheme has only a great national object in
view, and has no relation to private perſons, debtor
or creditor; nor can it, in any manner, affect private dealings. The emiſſion paſſing at par with

C   coin,

coin, will be received by creditors in general; and will also answer all the purposes of domestic commerce. We think the emission will not depreciate, because the paper is circulated on a pledge above twice its value, and therefore the borrower will not part with it under its nominal worth; and because the value of all commodities, even of gold and silver, depends on the quantity and *use or demand* for them. We are of opinion, that if any government should direct its taxes to be paid in paper money, it would thereby acquire a certain value, even though the term of its final redemption should depend altogether upon the pleasure of the government; if issued on *private* security, and receivable in taxes, it may add to its value in the opinion of the public. By the plan, the uses created for the paper exceed the quantity in circulation, and the *taxes alone* can easily employ and absorb the whole; and the sum annually decreases very considerably, by the sinking annually one-twentieth of the capital, and one half of the interest.

The senate have differed in sentiment from us, and are opposed to any emission *on loan*. They have submitted the reasons for their opinion to your consideration, as we now submit ours, and you will give them such weight as you think they deserve. It appears to us, that the senate have assigned but one objection to an emission of paper money *on loan*, to wit, that it will depreciate: They have enumerated a great number of causes

in

in support of their opinion, but it can only be a matter of judgment, to be determined by the event after trial. It is very clear to us, that if the money should depreciate, it cannot, in any manner, injure individuals; and we are not able to discover how the depreciation supposed (say five, ten, fifteen, or even twenty per cent. for argument sake) can injure our government. Let it be ad-mitted, that £100,000 brought into the treasury by taxes; should purchase tobacco and flour only worth £80,000 in gold and silver, this deficiency must be made up by a further tax, but the state will neither be richer or poorer. Suppose a man owes two silver dollars for his tax, for which he must give three bushels of wheat, if no paper money; but if there is, he can procure two paper dollars for two bushels of wheat; will he increase or dimi-nish his property by this circumstance? Why should paper money in this state depreciate more than in New-York or Pennsylvania, if emitted on as good a plan as in those states? In New-York the paper is issued *on loan, on land security;* and it passes at par with gold and silver, unless for the purchase of these metals for exportation, when the difference is two and a half per cent. In Pennsylvania their paper is issued *for taxes,* and passes current, ex-cept in the purchase of specie, in which case a dif-ference is made from five to ten per cent. Both these governments are acknowledged to be in the most flourishing circumstances as to trade and

C 2   wealth,

wealth, and the moft happy confequences have flow-ed from their paper emiffions, both to the public and the individual.

It is objected by the fenate, that our bill takes away the fpecie tax of 10s. which was applied to the ufe of congrefs, and alfo the fupplies of fpecie arifing from duties, two-thirds of which were appropriated to congrefs.

We admit, that our bill directed the emiffion to be taken in payment of the faid tax, and of the faid duties; and in reply to thefe objections, and to all the arguments ufed to fhew that a paper emiffion will deprive congrefs, and this ftate, of fpecie fupplies, we obferve, that the fyftem of taxation which we have hitherto adopted, is declared by congrefs to be *totally ineffectual*, and, if purfued, muft endanger the exiftence of the confederation. This ftate, on examination and inquiry, is found, on the fyftem hitherto purfued, among the moft deficient in complying with the requifition of congrefs. Although the paper emiffion was made receivable for taxes in all cafes, yet in all probability a confiderable fum would be neceffarily paid in gold and filver, becaufe the demand of money for taxes and duties for fees of office, fines, forfeitures, and licences, exceeds the quantity of paper which will be in circulation at any one time. And with the paper thus paid for taxes, under the management of a proper revenue officer, the produce of our country might be purchafed up, and fupplies pro-

cured

cured of gold and filver treble the fums produced
by our former fyftems of taxes and duties.

It is objected alfo by the fenate, that our bill in-
troduces a tax of paper money for ten years, and
fufpends all taxes in fpecie for that period. This
is a very miftaken conftruction of our bill. The
emiffion is receivable in all taxes, and when received it lies in the treafury fubject to the difpofi-
tion of the general affembly. From the exprefs
terms and provifions therefore of the bill, the circulation may ceafe at any period the general affembly fhall think proper. The fenate in their
meffage exprefs their defire of an emiffion for the
purpofe only of purchafing liquidated continental
fecurities. This propofal from the fenate we could
neither agree to, nor confer on, without giving up
the privilege of originating all money matters,
which privilege is granted to, and exclufively vefted
in us by the conftitution. We have already ex-
plained that *one* of the *principal* objects of the emiffion propofed by us was, to obtain the *means* of
procuring thefe continental fecurities. There is
this manifeft difference between the emiffion propofed by us, and that propofed by the fenate. By
our plan the money was *firft* to circulate *on loan,*
and every man, having land in fee, would have
an opportunity of borrowing. By the propofal of
the fenate, the money was only to be taken out by
the holders of the continental depreciated fecurities,
and every perfon wanting this money for taxes,

could

could only borrow from them. Every objection from depreciation applies with greater force to an emiſſion only to redeem final ſettlements, than to an emiſſion to anſwer *all* the purpoſes of taxation, and the payment of officers and lawyers fees, which alone would require a great part of the ſum in circulation. It appeared to us, that acceding to the ſcheme of emiſſion to purchaſe final ſettlements, though it might greatly benefit the *adventurers* in theſe ſecurities, would not anſwer any great *public* purpoſe, and if it could, that it might be better effected by the emiſſion on our plan; and it alſo appeared to us, that if we agreed to this ſcheme, it would effectually prevent an emiſſion *on loan* for ſeveral years.

Having thus deviſed a ſyſtem to relieve you in the payment of your taxes, and by the ſaid ſyſtem opened a loan-office, as the beſt means in our power to enable the induſtrious and enterpriſing to purſue their labours with ſpirit, vigour and effect, we turned our attention to the ſituation and circumſtances of debtors. The plan on which the paper emiſſion was propoſed to be iſſued, left it optional with the creditor to take or refuſe it; there was no legal obligation or force to take it on the principle of a tender for private debts: It was therefore eventual only, that this emiſſion would afford any relief at all to the debtor; if happily it did not depreciate, the creditor no doubt would then take

take it, and confequently the debtor would thereby be relieved.

· But the combined preffure of debts and taxes bore fo hard upon the debtor, that we conceived fome fure and certain relief ought, if poffible, to be devifed and adopted. Our courts of juftice, it appeared, were filled with lawfuits, and it was generally admitted that there was not enough of gold and filver to pay taxes, much lefs to pay both taxes and private debts. In deliberating on the fubject we found it both delicate and difficult. While we felt a real concern for the debtor, whofe diftrefs was in many inftances occafioned by the calamities of the late war, and heightened immediately on the peace by the neceffary impofition of heavy taxes, to pay off the national debt contracted during the war, we could not but be fenfible at the fame time of the critical fituation of the creditor, whofe engagements and profpects might be defeated by a fufpenfion of debts. The treaty too was a circumftance which very much embarraffed and perplexed us.

On a review of our laws as to the legal remedy the creditor had againft the debtor, we found he had his election to take the body of his debtor, or his lands, goods and chattels. If he took his execution againft the property of the debtor, the law authorized an appraifement of it on oath, and obliged him to take the property at fuch appraifement, but the election as to fpecies of property was

given

given to the creditor. The law, which made this provision on execution against the goods and chattels of the debtor, was an act passed in 1716 under the old government, and by the statute of fifth of George the second, extended here, and adopted before the revolution, lands were put on the footing of goods and chattels as to executions for debts.

On this review we conceived, that if executions against the body could be suspended for a time, and the creditor obliged to take substantial property for his debt at its actual worth, a relief would be given to the debtor, and as much attention preserved to the creditor and treaty as circumstances and the necessity of the case would admit. It appeared to us, that in most cases the debtor had enough of solid property to pay his debts, his distresses and difficulties arose from the acknowledged scarcity of gold and silver, and the impracticability of commanding it on a public sale of his property in any proportion to its real worth, and in such cases the creditor to avoid the taking of property under the act of 1716, took out execution against the person of the debtor, and locked him up in a gaol; the debtor, to relieve himself from the distresses, horrors and calamities of imprisonment, had no other means left but by a public sale of his property for gold and silver.

As the difficulties of the debtor arose principally from the present scarcity of gold and silver, and not from a want of sufficient property of the debtor, we framed

framed a bill fuited to the necessity of our affairs, giving it a duration only of one year.

By this bill, to the abstracts of which we refer you, the debtor in all cases may, on execution issued against him, discharge the same by property to be valued by sworn appraifers: But lest such property might prove no satisfaction to the creditor from any particular circumstances he might be under; the bill provided, that on all judgments, whether upon actions brought, or hereafter to be brought, if the creditor shall forbear to sue out execution, the debtor shall forbear to discharge the debt by property.

This bill is a system not adopted of choice; it is not devised as a fit or proper system for a permanent administration of justice, between creditor and debtor; we do not approve of it as such, or bring it forward to your view to be considered in that point of light. Such a system permanently established, would never suit a commercial country, nor operate either as an effectual or perfect administration of justice. We have adopted it on the principles only of necessity, resulting from the present embarrassed circumstances of the people, occasioned by the scarcity of gold and silver. It is a system merely calculated to meet the difficulties of the present times, and its duration was therefore temporary and limited to one year only. Considered on this ground, we trust it will meet with your approbation. But this bill also was rejected by the fenate.

The

The Appeal of the fenate, and of this houfe is *now* made to you as to the propriety and neceffity of an emiffion of *paper money circulated on loan, for the purpofe of enabling you to pay the heavy but neceffary taxes for the fupport of your own and the federal government*; and we wifh you to exprefs your fentiments to both branches of your legiflature. Under the prefent circumftances of our trade, and the heavy incumbrance of your debts to the ftate and individuals, we are of opinion, that you cannot annually pay, and that too conftantly and perpetually, the fum of £116,000 in *gold* and *filver*. As the impofing taxes on you muft always originate in this houfe, we were apprehenfive if we laid fuch heavy taxes on you, payable *only in gold and filver*, which we think is very fcarce, and bears no proportion to the amount of the taxes, that you would compare us to the Egyptian tafk-mafters who compelled the Ifraelites to make bricks without ftraw. If you entertain a different opinion from us, and think you can pay the neceffary taxes *in gold and filver*, be pleafed to fignify your pleafure, and we will immediately proceed to pafs laws for the collecting the fums neceffary for the fupport of this government, and alfo to defray your proportion of the charges of the federal union.

Signed by order of the Houfe of Delegates,

THOMAS COOKEY DEYE, Speaker.

PAPER

PAPER, Nº I.

100 0 0	one twentieth	5 0 0	six per cent.	6 0 0	paid in	11 0 0	sunk	8 0 0	in circulation	92 0 0
98 0 0		4 18 0		5 17 7		10 15 7		7 16 10½		84 3 1½
96 0 8½		4 16 0½		5 15 3		10 11 3½		7 13 8		76 9 5½
94 2 5½		4 14 1½		5 12 11		10 7 0½		7 10 7		68 18 10½
92 4 7¼		4 12 3		5 10 8		10 2 11		7 7 7		61 11 3
90 7 8¾		4 10 4½		5 8 5½		9 18 10		7 4 7		54 6 7¾
88 11 7		4 8 7		5 6 3½		9 14 10½		7 1 8½		47 4 11
86 16 2		4 6 9½		5 4 2		9 10 11½		6 18 10½		40 6 0½
85 1 5½		4 5 1		5 2 1		9 7 2		6 16 1¼		33 9 11¼
831 4 7	at five per cent.	41 11 3	six per cent.	49 17 5	11 per cent.	91 8 8		66 10 0¼	principal.	
		49 17 5	interest.					33 9 11¾	in circulation.	
		91 8 8	principal and interest paid in.					100 0 0		

Due the state at the expiration of the ninth year,	£ 83 7 5¾
In circulation at the expiration of the ninth year,	33 9 11¾
Gained by the state	49 17 6

PAPER

P A P E R, No II.

Capital	paid 1-20th	6 per cent.	paid in	funk	in circulation
250 00 0 0	12500 0 0	15000 0 0	27500 0 0	20000 0 0	230000 0 0
245 00 0 0	12250 0 0	14700 0 0	26950 0 0	19600 0 0	210400 0 0
240100 0 0	12005 0 0	14406 0 0	26411 0 0	19208 0 0	191192 0 0
235298 0 0	11764 18 0	14117 17 7	25882 15 7	18823 16 9½	172368 3 2½
230592 0 10	11529 12 0	13835 10 5	25365 2 5	18447 8 2½	153920 16 0
225980 1 0	11299 0 0	13558 16 1	24857 16 1	18078 8 1½	135842 7 10½
221460 9 0	11073 0 5½	13387 12 6	24360 12 11½	17716 16 8½	118125 11 2
217931 4 10	10851 11 3	13021 17 6	23873 8 9	17362 10 0	100763 1 2
212 90 12 4	10614 10 8	12761 8 8½	23395 19 4½	17015 5 0	83747 16 2

£ 2078152 8 0 at 5 p.c.   103907 12 4½ 6 per cent.   124689 15 2 9½ 11 p.c.   228596 15 2 8 p.c. 166252 3 10   the sum funk.

124689 2 9½ interest paid in.   83747 16 2 in circulation.

228596 15 2 interest and principal paid in.   250000 0 0

Due the state at the expiration of the ninth year,   208436 16 0
In circulation at the expiration of the ninth year,   83747 16 2
Gained by the state,   £ 124688 19 10

The proof and plan is simply this; though five per cent. principal, and six per cent. interest, (being eleven per cent.) is paid in annually, and the sum in circulation reduced eight per cent. the capital or debt to the state is reduced but two per cent. annually.

A Note by the English Editor.——The Difference between Stirling and Currency, is 66 two-thirds per Cent. and consequently the Dollar is considered as 4s. 6d. or 7s. 6d.——The Project of PAPER-MONEY was finally relinquished.

F I N I S.

NEW BOOKS printed for JOHN STOCK-DALE, PICCADILLY.

AN ESTIMATE of the COMPARATIVE STRENGTH of GREAT BRITAIN, during the prefent and four preceding Reigns; and of the Loffes of her Trade from every War fince the Revolution, New modelled and continued to 1785. By GEORGE CHALMERS, Efq; Price 3s. 6d. fewed, or 5s. Calf, lettered.

The DEBATES of the LORDS and COMMONS, during the Fourth Seffion of the Sixteenth Parliament of Great Britain. Elegantly printed in Three Volumes, Octavo. Price 1l. 1s. half bound and lettered.

Alfo the DEBATES of the Firft, Second, and Third Seffions, Three Volumes each Set. Price 1l. 1s.

And the DEBATES of the Laft Seffion of the late Parliament, in Six Volumes, Octavo. Price 1l. 11s. 6d. half bound and lettered.

A COLLECTION of ORIGINAL ROYAL LETTERS, written by King Charles the Firft and Second, King James the Second, and the King and Queen of Bohemia. Together with ORIGINAL LETTERS, written by Prince Rupert, Charles Louis Count Palatine, the Duchefs of Hanover, and feveral other diftinguifhed Perfons, from the Year 1619 to 1665. Dedicated with Permiffion to his Majefty. By Sir GEORGE BROMLEY, Bart. (Ornamented with elegant Engravings, from original Paintings by Cooper, Sir Peter Lely, &c. executed by Meffrs. Sherwins, of the Queen of Bohemia, Emanuel Scrope Howe, Prince Rupert, and Ruperta, natural Daughter of Prince Rupert; and a Plate of Autographs and Seals.) In One Volume, Price 10s. 6d. in Boards.

NOTES on the STATE of VIRGINIA. By his Excellency THOMAS JEFFERSON, Minifter Plenipotentiary from the United States to the Court of France. In One Volume, Octavo, Price 7s. in Boards, illuftrated with a large Map, comprehending the whole of Virginia, Maryland, Delaware, and Penfylvania, with Parts of feveral other of the United States of America.

The HISTORY of NEW HOLLAND, from its firft Difcovery in 1616, to the prefent Time. To which is prefixed, An Introductory Difcourfe on Banifhment. By the
Right

BOOKS printed for JOHN STOCKDALE.

Right Hon. WILLIAM EDEN. Illuftrated with a Map of New Holland, a Chart of Botany Bay, and a general Chart from England to Botany Bay. Price 6s. in Boards.

An ESSAY, containing Strictures on the Union of Scotland with England, and on the prefent Situation of Ireland; being an Introduction to De Foe's Hiftory of the Union. By J. L. DE LOLME, Adv. Price 3s. 6d. fewed, containing 95 Pages in Quarto.

The HISTORY of the UNION between ENGLAND and SCOTLAND; with a Collection of Original Papers relating thereto. By the celebrated DANIEL DE FOE. With the above Introduction, in which the Confequences and Probability of a like Union between this Country and Ireland are confidered, by JOHN LEWIS DE LOLME, Author of the Work on the Conftitution of England. To which is prefixed a LIFE of the AUTHOR, and a copious INDEX. In one large Volume Quarto, containing One Thoufand Pages, Price 1l. 10s. in Boards.

The BEAUTIES of the BRITISH SENATE; taken from the Debates of the Lords and Commons, from the Beginning of the Adminiftration of Sir Robert Walpole, to the End of the Second Seffion of the Right Hon. William Pitt. Being an impartial Selection of, or faithful Extracts from, the moft eminent Speeches, delivered in the Courfe of a moft important and truly interefting Period of more than fixty Years, feverally arranged under their refpective Heads, with the Names of the Members, to whom they are afcribed, annexed thereto. To which is prefixed, The LIFE of Sir Robert WALPOLE. In Two Volumes, Octavo. Price 10s. 6d. in Boards, or 12s. bound in Calf and lettered.

HISTORICAL TRACTS. By Sir JOHN DAVIES, Attorney-General, and Speaker of the Houfe of Commons in Ireland; confifting of, 1. A Difcovery of the true Caufe why Ireland was never brought under Obedience of the Crown of England. 2. A Letter to the Earl of Salifbury, on the State of Ireland in 1607. 3. A Letter to the Earl of Salifbury in 1610, giving an Account of the Plantation in Ulfter. 4. A Speech to the Lord Deputy in 1613, tracing the ancient Conftitution of Ireland. To which is prefixed, a new Life of the Author, from authentic Documents. In One Volume Octavo, Price 5s. in Boards, or 6s. in Calf, and lettered.

A

BOOKS printed by JOHN STOCKDALE.

A BRIEF ESSAY on the ADVANTAGES and DIS-ADVANTAGES which refpectively attend France and Great-Britain with regard to Trade. By Jofiah Tucker, D. D. Dean of Gloucefter. Price 2s.

POEMS on VARIOUS SUBJECTS, By Henry Jamea Pye, Efq; M. P. Elegantly printed in Two Volumes, 8vo. and embellifhed with beautiful Frontifpieces, Price 12s. in Boards.

STOCKDALE's EDITION of SHAKESPEARE; in-cluding, in One Volume, 8vo. the WHOLE of his DRA-MATIC WORKS; with Explanatory Notes, compiled from various Commentators. To which are prefixed his LIFE and WILL. Price only 15s.

And the WORKS of Dr. SAMUEL JOHNSON, in 13 Vols. Price 3l. 18s. in Boards, or elegantly Calf, gilt, 4l. 17s. 6d. The 12th and 13th Volumes may be had feparate, Price 12s. in Boards.

N. B. The 14th Volume of the above Works is in the Prefs, and will be publifhed in a few Days.

The HISTORY of SANDFORD and MERTON: A work intended for the Ufe of Children. Embellifhed with beautiful Frontifpieces, in 2 vols. price 6s. 6d. bound.

Captain COOK's THIRD and LAST VOYAGE to the PACIFICK OCEAN, in the years 1776, 1777, 1778, 1779, and 1780. Faithfully abridged from the quarto edi-tion, publifhed by order of his Majefty; illuftrated with copper-plates. Price 4s. bound.

A COMPLETE GEOGRAPHICAL DICTIONARY, or UNIVERSAL GAZETTEER, of Ancient and Mo-dern Geography, containing a full, particular, and accurate Defcription of the known World, in Europe, Afia, Africa, aud America; comprifing a complete fyftem of geography, illuftrated with correct maps and beautiful views of the prin-cipal cities, &c. and chronological tables of the Sovereigns of Europe. The geographical parts by John Sealy, A. M. Member of the Roman Academy; author of the Hiftoire Chronologique, facrée et profane; Elements of Geography and Aftronomy, &c. &c. interfperfed with extracts from the private manufcripts of one of the officers who accompanied Captain Cook in his voyage to the Southern Hemifphere. The aftronomical parts from the papers of the late Mr. Ifrael

Lyons,

BOOKS printed by JOHN STOCKDALE.

Lyons, of Cambridge, aftronomer in Lord Mulgrave's voyage to the Northern Hemifphere. In two large volumes, 4to. elegantly bound in calf, gilt, and lettered. Price 2l. 2s. or 1l. 11s. 6d. in boards.

ARTICLES of CHARGE of HIGH CRIMES and MISDEMEANORS againſt Warren Haſtings, Eſq; prefented to the Houfe of Commons by the Right Hon. Edmund Burke. In one large vol. 8vo. Price 7s. in boards.

The DEFENCE of WARREN HASTINGS, Eſq; (late Governor General of Bengal,) at the bar of the Houfe of Commons, upon the matter of the feveral Charges of High Crimes and Mifdemeanors, prefented againſt him in the year 1786. In one vol. 8vo. Price 5s. in boards.

MINUTES of the EVIDENCE before the HOUSE of COMMONS, relative to the Charges brought againſt Warren Haſtings, Eſq. In one volume. Price 5s. in boards.

The CONSTITUTIONS of the feveral INDEPENDENT STATES of AMERICA; with a Preface and Dedication to the Duke of Portland. By the Rev. William Jackfon. In one vol. 8vo. Price 6s. in boards.

The HISTORY of the REVOLUTION of SOUTH CAROLINA, from a Britifh Province to an Independent State. By David Ramfay, M. D. Ornamented with maps and charts. In two vols. 8vo. Price 12s. in boards.

Lightning Source UK Ltd.
Milton Keynes UK
UKHW021039110119
335297UK00012B/1749/P